Nine Miles to Mammoth Cave

The Story of the Mammoth Cave Railroad

Nine Miles to Mammoth Cave

The Story of the Mammoth Cave Railroad

Colleen O'Connor Olson

Cave Books
www.cavebooks.com

Dayton, Ohio

Library of Congress Control Number 2012032219
ISBN 978-0-939748-78-5

First Edition December, 2012

Library of Congress Cataloging-in-Publication Data

Olson, Colleen O'Connor, 1966-
Nine miles to Mammoth Cave : the story of the Mammoth Cave Railroad / Colleen O'Connor Olson. -- First edition.
    pages cm
Includes index.
ISBN 978-0-939748-78-5 (pbk. : alk. paper) -- ISBN 0-939748-78-9 (pbk. : alk. paper)
1. Mammoth Cave Railroad--History. 2. Railroads--Kentucky--History. I. Title.

TF25.M36O47 2012
385.09769'752--dc23

2012032219

Published by CAVE BOOKS
4700 Amberwood Drive
Dayton, Ohio 45424-4602
http://www.cavebooks.com

CAVE BOOKS is the publications affiliate of the Cave Research Foundation

Publisher: Roger McClure
Editors: Elizabeth Winkler, Paul Steward, Tom Rea
Layout: Tom Rea, Greyhound Press
Cover Graphic Design: Greyhound Press
Front Cover photograph: Hercules and passengers on the Mammoth Cave Railroad.
Back Cover drawing: A color print of the train stopped enroute.

©2012 Colleen O'Connor Olson

All rights reserved. This book or any parts thereof may not be reproduced in any form without written permission.

Printed in the United States of America

Table of Contents

Introduction   3
The L&N Railroad   7
Working on the Mammoth Cave Railroad   9
Travel Before the Railroad   19
How Horses Lost their Jobs   21
"All Aboard!"   25
The Passengers   29
Where Are We Going?   33
Doing Business   47
A Railroad Retires   53
A National Park and a New Life for a Train   55
A Facelift for the New Millennium   59
Remembering the Mammoth Cave Railroad   61
Want More Trains?   63
Lots of Thanks   65
Notes   67
Index   73

Nine Miles to Mammoth Cave

Note from a Mammoth Cave Park Ranger and Writer

I first came to Mammoth Cave National Park in 1992 on a Greyhound bus. I had just graduated from college and was seeking adventure and a job with the National Park Service. I eventually found both. When I arrived at the park, I saw an unusual old train displayed by the camp store and asked a Mammoth Cave Hotel maintenance man about it. "Oh, that's Hercules," he said.

I soon learned that a little train with this mythical name brought tourists to the cave in the old days, but my curiosity about the details had to wait. My new job as an interpretive ranger and guide kept me busy learning about the cave—there's so much to know, I'm still learning 20 years later.

After mastering basic cave guide survival techniques (like lighting lanterns when the power fails and explaining to fourth graders why bats don't fly into rocks) I found time to seek out the story behind the little railroad that ran 9 miles from Park City to Mammoth Cave. Here is what I discovered.

Colleen O'Connor Olson
Mammoth Cave, Kentucky, 2011

The Question:
How could a cave earn its own railroad?

Atchison, Topeka & Santa Fe; Union Pacific; Mammoth Cave – all are names of railroads. You can see why cities and an ocean would have railroads named for them, they're big and people want to go there, but a cave? How did a cave become so important that it warranted its own railroad?

The Answer:
By being Mammoth.

Famous for being the world's longest cave (390 miles as of 2011), Mammoth Cave is also known for its geology, archeology, diverse cave life, and history. It's a national park, a World Heritage site, and a biosphere reserve. Ralph Waldo Emerson, Herman Melville (he compared Moby Dick's mouth to the cave's entrance), and Jules Verne wrote about it. Whiskey, chewing tobacco, an auction house, a gas company, and an assortment of other businesses use the Mammoth Cave name. Over 400,000 eager visitors come to see it every year. But Mammoth Cave started out as just a hole in the ground.

For many millennia, only bats, cave crickets, eyeless cave fish, and other cave-dwelling animals adapted for such an inhospitable habitat entered or lived in the cave. People and most animals stayed above ground.

Then, about 4,000 years ago, American Indians cast the first light into what had been darkness for millions of years. These early cave explorers ventured into the cave by the light of cane reed torches to mine the mineral gypsum from the cave walls. They probably used the gypsum as a trade item, soil conditioner, or to make paint or plaster, no one knows for sure. They left torch fragments, slippers, tools, and other artifacts that the cave shielded from the elements and preserved for later generations to marvel over, speculate about, and study.

These ancient cavers mined and explored the cave off and on for about 2,000 years. No one knows why they stopped. For the next 1,800 years, bats and other cave animals had the place all to themselves.

According to a local legend, one day in the 1790s, the cave

Introduction

animals' tranquility ended with a clap of gunfire and a loud bellow. A hunter named John Houchin shot and wounded a bear and planned to capture his game even if it meant following the furious animal into a dark cave. We don't know whether John got his bear or not. This legend may be a bit exaggerated, but modern people first entered Mammoth Cave in the late 1700s and have been visiting it ever since.

Ordinarily, the cave wouldn't have interested many people, but saltpeter (the main ingredient in black gunpowder) drew saltpeter merchants to what otherwise would have been seen as just a hole in the ground. In the late 1700s and early 1800s, slaves worked long hours by lantern light to mine saltpeter from the cave dirt. The cave owners shipped the saltpeter to the DuPont Company in Delaware, where gunpowder makers mixed it with sulfur and charcoal to make black gunpowder. DuPont valued the high quality of the cave's saltpeter, and Mammoth became an important source of saltpeter for the War of 1812. Many other caves and rock shelters also contributed to the supply. Mining continued until 1815, when the end of the war made saltpeter mining no longer profitable. Mining never resumed, although the equipment still remains in the cave.

Even before the mining stopped, the cave drew curiosity seekers. "The Mammoth Cave is the most extensive and stupendous vault in the known world," wrote an anonymous traveler in 1815. A year later, the newspaper *Thomas's Massachusetts Spy* published his words.[1] Readers wanted to see this "stupendous vault" for themselves. Why not charge them money? Mammoth Cave joined Niagara Falls and Plymouth Rock as one of America's earliest tourist attractions.

At first, few tourists came. In his book *An Excursion Through The United States and Canada During the Years 1822–23*, William Blane wrote "scarcely any persons, except those engaged in the manufacture of saltpeter, have had the curiosity to visit the place." But he also called Mammoth Cave "the greatest natural curiosity in the Western States."[2] The more writers wrote, the more travelers flocked to this massive hole in the ground.

In the 1830s, the cave owners built a hotel to accommodate increasing numbers of visitors. Explorers discovered new passages and tour routes expanded. Cave guides led visitors by lantern light to Giant's Coffin, Fat Man's Misery, and the Star Chamber, destinations still popular today. Travelers gazed in awe at mammoth-size chambers, a seemingly bottomless pit, Indian drawings of zigzag and crisscross lines, and sparkling gypsum crystals that visitors compared to roses and snowballs (two very unrelated things, but that's how weird gypsum looks). In addition to the wonders of the cave, guests enjoyed fine dining, a ballroom, music, a tenpin alley, billiards, and croquet. Mammoth Cave's day as a full-fledged tourist destination had arrived.

The L&N Railroad

In 1832, some Kentuckians suggested building a railroad between Louisville, Kentucky, and Nashville, Tennessee. At first, Louisville's citizens didn't like the idea; boats on the Ohio River and dirt wagon roads had served their transportation needs since the city began, why would they need a railroad? But as other cities became connected by rail, the people of Louisville feared they'd be bypassed, making the idea of a railroad between the two cities popular. In 1850, the Commonwealth of Kentucky granted a charter to build a railroad from Louisville to the Tennessee state line; Tennessee granted a separate charter for the railroad to run on to Nashville.

Louisville's citizens were smart to jump on board. The Louisville and Nashville Railroad (the L&N) became important to transportation across the south. It began running between Louisville and Nashville in 1859. In time, it branched south to Birmingham, Atlanta, New Orleans, and Pensacola; west to Saint Louis and Memphis; and north to Cincinnati.[3] By the late 1800s, a town needed a railway station to thrive, but a rail stop didn't guarantee survival. The song *L&N Doesn't Stop Here Any More*, made popular by Johnny Cash, tells about a dying town the L&N no longer bothered to stop at.

The L&N stopped at Glasgow Junction (now called Park City), Kentucky, a tiny burg halfway between Louisville and Nashville. The town had about 75 people, three dry goods stores, a drug store, two saloons, a hotel, a church, a tobacco warehouse, a doctor, a lawyer, and a telegraph office, more businesses than it has today.[4] Glasgow Junction lacked the commerce and the population of the big cities along the L&N, yet, because it was near Mammoth Cave, many L&N passengers got off at the Glasgow Junction station. But after the train pulled away, tourists still had a rough 9-mile stagecoach ride to the cave. The modern luxury and speed of the train made the stagecoach seem archaic.

Conveyances will be ready upon the Arrival of Trains to Convey Passengers Either to

MAMMOTH CAVE

—OR—

Diamond Cave,

OR TO BOTH, AS MAY SUIT THE PLEASURE OF VISITORS.

Persons can visit Diamond Cave and take the "Short Route" in Mammoth Cave, and return to Glasgow Junction the same day, in time for the evening trains going North or South.

GOOD HOTEL ACCOMMODATIONS

—AT THE—

PROCTOR HOUSE,

Well known throughout the land as

BELL'S TAVERN.

Where persons wishing to visit the Caves, will be entertained with old fashioned Kentucky hospitality.

DIAMOND CAVE

Is provided with spacious stairways, substantial Railings and good walks throughout, so that all parts of this beautiful Cave can be visited by ladies and gentlemen in their travelling costumes.

Before the Mammoth Cave Railroad, L&N Railroad passengers got off the train at Glasgow Junction and rode the stage to Mammoth or Diamond Caves.

Working on the Mammoth Cave Railroad

"KENTUCKY'S CAVES. They are to be connected with the outer world by railroad—something that should have been done long ago," said an article in the August 17, 1877, edition of the Louisville *Courier-Journal*. The paper announced that a party of "men of wealth and influence" from Louisville traveled by train to Cave City and by stagecoach to Mammoth Cave and nearby Proctor Cave to explore the possibility of building a railroad to the caves.[5] By the 1870s, stagecoaches were old-fashioned; if tourists could travel to Mammoth and other local show caves faster and more comfortably by train, tourism would increase.

In 1874, hotel and show cave owner Colonel Larkin J. Proctor, Colonel R.H. Lacey (eventual president of the Mammoth Cave Railroad), Colonel Edmund W. Cole, Jere Baxter, Colonel Overton Lea, A.M. Overton, and J. Hill Eakin (the first Mammoth Cave Railroad president) incorporated the Mammoth Cave Railroad (M.C.R.R.)[6]

But nothing happened. At least not at first. People waiting to hear the train whistle take the place of horse's hooves got impatient. Finally, the June 14, 1886, edition of The Glasgow *Weekly Times* said:

> The first load of ties for the Mammoth Cave Railroad were hauled today by Mr. Scott Coats ... . There is no doubt of the certainty of the road now, and we believe it to be a matter of but a few months until trains will be running. It is difficult to understand why an enterprise like this was not undertaken and carried out long ago ... .[7]

The Mammoth Cave Construction Company began building the railroad in July. Henry Chapman, a farmer and chimney builder from near Mammoth Cave, and Jim McDaniel started laying 8.7 miles of track from Glasgow Junction to the cave.[8]

Some track facts: the Mammoth Cave Railroad's rails weighed 56 pounds per yard, typical for spur railroads; long distance rails tend to

In spite of hilly terrain, the railroad had only one trestle.

weigh 139 pounds per yard to support bigger trains. The M.C.R.R. gauge, or width between the rails, was the standard 4 feet, 8½ inches. The right-of-way was the usual 25 feet on each side of the tracks. The hilly terrain and desire to avoid the expense of road cuts and too many trestles (the railroad had only one 50-foot trestle) resulted in the grade being as much as 4%,* a steep climb for a little engine.[9]

The L&N Railroad, the Mammoth Cave Railroad's link to everywhere else, agreed to lease the new railroad for 25 years from the date of completion. L&N knew tourism was good for the passenger train business; the railroad even owned a show cave called Colossal Cavern near Mammoth Cave. L&N supplied the rolling stock (a railroad term for cars) free of charge.[10] At first, one or two L&N engines ran on the M.C.R.R., but in 1888 they bought four used dummy locomotives especially for the little railroad.

---

*   On a 4% grade the elevation increases 4 feet for every 100 feet traveled. This pushes the limit for most trains; steeper terrain requires a special railroad called a cog railroad.

Working on the Mammoth Cave Railroad

A Little Dummy History

The term "dummy" is a compliment not an insult; dummy engines were relatively quiet, or dumb, compared to most locomotives.†

The Gloucester & Cheltenham Railway in England made the first dummy locomotive in 1831. Henry Waterman built the first American dummy engine for the Hudson River Railroad in New York City.

New Yorkers didn't like the dirty, black soot; rumbling noise; and stench of burning coal of steam trains, so the city's train depot was on the edge of town. But having the railroad away from downtown meant railroad passengers had the inconvenience of riding 3 miles by horse-drawn carriage between the train depot and the downtown depot. Waterman believed a cleaner, quieter engine could quickly take passengers downtown without subjecting townspeople to smoke and soot. Instead of coal, Waterman's dummy burned coke (distilled coal), making it cleaner and quieter than other locomotives. As coal bakes into coke, the tar, gasses, and light oil bake out. Burning coke

Though the dummy is disguised as a car, steam rising from the tack gives away its true identity as an engine.

---

† Even with a quiet dummy engine, trains rolling on tracks make noise. In the May, 1909, issue of *Scientific American*, Horace Hovey, a professor who wrote a lot about caves, reported that while in a Mammoth Cave chamber called Chief City "... we plainly heard the steam cars running overhead along the Mammoth Cave Railroad."

11

emits little smoke. The dummy doesn't look like a typical locomotive either; its gears and moving parts are disguised to make it look more like a passenger car than an engine. Even people who objected to locomotives on city streets hardly recognized the dummy as a locomotive.

In spite of the dummy's more genteel sound and appearance, people favored horse-drawn railway cars over engines for public transportation in cities. Cincinnati tried dummy engines on the streets in 1860, but horses were reluctant to pass them, so the city abandoned the plan. Philadelphia used the engines during the 1876 Centennial Exposition, but they damaged tracks built for lighter horse-drawn railcars, and cost more to run than the horse-drawn cars. After a year, Philly lost its brotherly love for the dummy engine.

Although unpopular in inner-cities, dummy engines became common on suburban railways; about 80 railways used them in the 1890s.

The dummy engine's heyday was short. By the beginning of the 20th century, electric street cars replaced most of the little locomotives. The electric street cars didn't last long either; automobiles soon took over. The Mammoth Cave Railroad engines, probably the last dummy engines in America, were retired in 1929.

The Mammoth Cave Railroad engine displayed near the camp store at Mammoth Cave National Park doesn't run, but is the best preserved dummy engine in North America, maybe in the world. Of about a thousand dummies made in the U.S., only six others still exist, none of which run. They haven't received the same loving care as Mammoth Cave's engine, so are less pristine.[11] You can see three of the other surviving dummies on display at Penetanguishene Centennial Museum and Archives in Penetanguishene, Ontario; Fort Worden State Park in Port Townsend, Washington; and Sharlot Hall Museum in Prescott, Arizona.

Hercules the Tank Engine

If you have small children, you may be asked, "What makes Thomas the Tank Engine a tank engine?" (For those of you with no little boys in your life, Thomas is a wildly popular toy tank engine with a huge fan base.) Parents and grandparents who are not train buffs spend much time pondering over the tank engine question.

Most American engines were tender locomotives, meaning they

Working on the Mammoth Cave Railroad

Like all tank engines, the Mammoth Cave Railroad dummies didn't need to pull tender cars, their coal bins and water tanks were built in.

pulled a tender or coal car that carried fuel (usually coal) and water to make steam to power the engine. Like Thomas the Tank Engine, the dummy engines used on the M.C.R.R. had no tenders, they were tank engines, meaning the water tank and coal bin were part of the locomotive. Unable to carry as much fuel as a tender locomotive, tank engines traveled only short distances.

To power the tank engine, the fireman shoveled coal from the coal bin behind the cab into the fire box under the cab. The fire heated water in the boiler, creating steam pressure that drove pistons that moved the main rods and connecting rods attached to the driver wheels, making them go around.

Baldwin Locomotive Works in Philadelphia built the Mammoth Cave Railroad's five 0-4-2T dummy engines in 1888. Train-talk translation: the model number 0-4-2T means the engine has no pilot wheels, four driver wheels, and two trailing wheels. The pilot, or front wheels help guide the engine and keep it on the tracks when going around curves, important for big engines, but less so for little dummies. The driver wheels, located under the boiler, are powered by the engine and support most of the weight. The trailing wheels under the cab help support and distribute the engine's weight.

The M.C.R.R. dummies served short stints on street railways on the Nashville & West Nashville Railroad and the East End Railway in Memphis before coming to Mammoth Cave.

All the engines had numbers to identify them but only one,

13

The engine Hercules — small, but mighty.

Hercules, had a name. In Greek and Roman mythology, the strong man Hercules was half god, half mortal: the son of the god Zeus (or his Roman counterpart Jupiter) and a mortal woman.

Hercules was popular—writers wrote about the little dummy and photographers took its picture, showing off the name boldly painted on the engine's side. When the original Hercules engine broke down beyond repair, railroad workers painted the same name and number on its replacement.[12] People often called the whole train Hercules, regardless of which engine pulled it. The mighty name implied strength, but not everyone thought the name fit the locomotive. A local man named Jewell Furlong wrote:

> The name "Hercules" was a laugh. The little train, when heavily loaded, would stall on every steep grade. Then, as folklore has it, the conductor would go through the coaches yelling, "First-class passengers, please take your seats; second-class passengers, please get off and walk; third-class passengers, please get off and push!"[13]

In the dummies' defense, they were built for flat suburban streets, not steep terrain.

Each locomotive had two cow catchers (railroad workers use the more dignified term pilot). The cow catcher did just what the name implies: knocked cows or other obstacles off the tracks to protect the locomotive, similar to a car's bumper. The engines sometimes ran in reverse, so they had cow catchers in back as well as in front to remove obstacles when going either way.

The ability to run backward and forward also required a headlight on each end of the engines. Carbide powered the lights, quite befitting a train traveling to a cave, carbide also fueled caving lights for many years. Cave explorers and railroad men liked the carbide light for the same reasons, it is brighter than a lantern and puts out a pleasant, pale yellow light that can be reflected and focused in a way lantern light can't be. Although lanterns are inferior to carbide lights, cave explorers and railroad men also used lanterns, because until the late 1800s, that's all they had. Twenty-first century railroads have forsaken carbide lights, but some nostalgic cave explorers still use them.

A carbide light has two chambers, the upper one for water, and the lower one for carbide. The water drips onto the carbide, creating acetylene gas to fuel a flame. A reflector behind the flame reflects the light, making the much desired bright headlight.

Along with the engines, L&N supplied four red wooden cars; two combination coaches and two passenger coaches. Combination coaches, or combines, have a passenger section and a separate section for luggage or freight. Eliminating the need for a separate baggage car made combines popular on trains traveling short distances. The passenger coaches, one long and one short, just carried people. The wooden seats had no cushions—not too comfy, but the ride was short. A coal stove in each car kept passengers warm in the winter.[14]

Today, you can see an engine and a combine coach on display at Mammoth Cave National Park.

For maintenance, workers had a small hand car like those in old western movies. Much to the delight of local kids, the car was stored unsecured at Newt France's store in a community called Union City. Former Mammoth Cave guide Coy Hanson told me that as a kid he and his friends would "borrow" the hand car for nighttime rides. Coy said riding downhill was fun, but pushing the car back up was hard work.[15]

Link and pin couplers, universally used in the early days of railroads, connected the engines and the cars.[16] To join cars, a moving car rolled up to a stationary car, where a railroad worker stood between them to put the pin in the joining links. Many railroad men lost fingers (or worse) doing this. By the 1880s, safer coupling methods existed, so the link and pin design became less common. Mammoth Cave Railroad workers still used the dangerous link and

15

pin but apparently escaped serious injury.

The M.C.R.R. didn't need many facilities. The L&N Railroad shared their depot in Glasgow Junction with the little railroad. The M.C.R.R. had its own water tanks in Glasgow Junction and Mammoth Cave, a small freight house at the cave, and a repair shed in Glasgow Junction.[17] The railroad lacked a coal shed, so coal for the locomotives was dumped in a pile at Glasgow Junction where, some say, locals helped themselves to the supply.[18]

As long as the L&N leased the M.C.R.R., the larger railroad supplied a wye (pronounced like the letter Y) to turn the train around at Mammoth Cave.[19] A railroad wye has tracks that form a triangle, so a train can pull up on one side of the triangle, back onto another side at a corner, then pull forward onto the third side to face the direction it came from. The L&N removed the wye around 1900

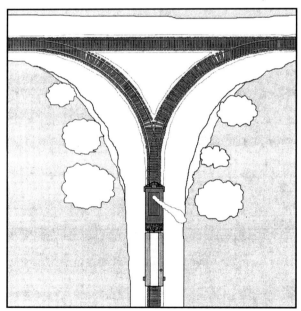

The wye allowed the train to turn around.

when the L&N ended its lease. The M.C.R.R. replaced the wye with run-around tracks at both ends of the line. With run-around tracks, workers could pull the train off the main track, unhook the engine from the cars, back the engine up on the main track so it would be on the other end of the train, and reattach the cars. Thus, the engine ran in front of the cars when going either way, but the engine ran

Working on the Mammoth Cave Railroad

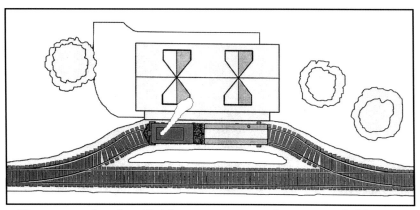

The run-around track enabled the engine to move to the opposite end of the train, but the engine had to run backwards on the return trip.

backwards on the trip back to Glasgow Junction.[20]

In spite of the 12-year delay between the incorporation of the railroad and actual construction in July of 1886, once work got going, it moved fast. The October 23, 1886, edition of *The Washington Post* announced the railroad would open in early November. An entry in the Mammoth Cave Estate Fees ledger says, "November 8th 1886 Monday, W.F. Richardson, U.S.A. 1st Passenger on M.C.R.R. 1350 3.00."[21] 1350 is military time for 1:50 P.M. (accurate time is important on railroads, that's why old pictures and movies often show the conductor checking his watch). Mr. Richardson's ticket cost $3.00.

The railroad leaders planned a big celebration for the opening; they invited Kentucky governor James Proctor Knott and every other state governor.[22] Alas, no governors showed up. Hardly anyone did. They canceled the formal ceremony due to the lack of interest, but the few people who did come "enjoyed an excellent dinner at the Cave Hotel," said the November 24, 1886, edition of *Hart County News*.[23]

Fourteen months later, cave visitor Oliver Doyle wrote and mailed a love letter from the Mammoth Cave Hotel to his sweetheart, Annie Pulliam, in Louisville. His romantic note from the cave worked; they got married. Fifty years later, Annie's son found the love letter in a pile of old Mammoth Cave pictures and brochures that his mom had carefully saved in a trunk. This romantic story is entertaining, but the real item of interest is the envelope Doyle mailed the love letter in. It bore an ad boasting of the modern convenience of the train:

17

Mammoth Cave Hotel. Open all year. W.C. Comstock, lessee. Quick time and close railroad connections. No more slow, tiresome stage ride. No delay.

The railroad meant that Mammoth and the surrounding show caves entered the 20th century in modern style.

Travel Before the Railroad

For several years, cave visitors arrived on horseback via roads that were little more than paths through the woods.

The Green River flows half a mile from Mammoth Cave, but prior to dams built in the early 1900s, it ran too shallow for large boats, so travelers couldn't ride to the cave on grand riverboats like the ones on the Mississippi and Ohio Rivers.

By the summer of 1833 (possibly earlier), stagecoach service from Glasgow Junction to the cave began.[24] Coach seats were comfier than a saddle, and the stage driver and the horses did the work, but the trip was still hard. Before the service began, some people predicted that the road was too rough for the stage. Even J.H. Harlow, the first man to drive a stage to Mammoth Cave, had doubts; he called the road to the cave an "ox-path." But Harlow and his passengers arrived safely.[25]

In the early 1840s, Mammoth Cave's owner, Dr John Croghan, persuaded local officials to build a better road from Cave City to the cave, a distance of about 10 miles.

Two stage services, one owned by D.L. Graves, the other by Andy McCoy, used this road. McCoy owned two Concord coaches, the Cadillac of its day. Four horses or mules drew the coaches, named the Florida and the John A. Bell (the coaches, not the horses).[26]

In spite of the improved road and fancy stagecoaches, the ride was still rough, even by 19th century standards. Albert Tissandier, a French artist traveling across America in 1885, wrote:

> Only the victims themselves can believe the number of dreadful bumps, holes and ruts in the road. ... the only thing to do is laugh heartily. The American ladies who were the ornaments of our little excursion were the first to give us the signal. They were delighted, and the more the wagon shook, the happier they seemed. We tried to ease the shocks and bumps by giving them our shawls and blankets, but they only burst out laughing again. It is

true that, although the roads don't exist so to speak, the country is charming."[27]

If the horses could not pull the stage through the mud or up a hill, passengers had to get out and walk.

The competition between the stagecoach businesses was as rough as the road. In 1873, stagecoach owner Andy McCoy attacked Dan Kelly, one of his rival's employees. Kelly sued McCoy for assault and battery and won $1,500 in damages.[28]

Stagecoach travel was also slow. The 9-mile ride from Bell's Tavern in Glasgow Junction took 3 hours, the train trip about one hour. Today the drive takes 15 minutes.[29]

How Horses Lost their Jobs

In the distant past, people had to walk to get anywhere. Then, about 4,000 to 5,000 years ago someone climbed on a wild horse and after much bucking and kicking made it do the walking. This probably looked dangerous and crazy to spectators, but it began a long relationship between humans and horses. Camels, donkeys, cattle, reindeer, dogs, and elephants have also been used for transportation, but for thousands of years, the horse was number one.

About 600 B.C., Greeks built a stone railroad called Diolkos across the Isthmus of Corinth to transport goods and boats on horse-drawn carts between the Corinthian and Saronic Gulfs.[30] At first, horses probably liked the railroad, the rails made pulling loads easier, but little did they know the Diolkos railroad was the beginning of the

The arrival of the railroad and automobiles didn't immediately put horses out of work, but their careers in transportation were nearing the end.

21

end of their reign as our favorite land transportation. Horses didn't lose their jobs immediately; it took another 2,400 years for machines to replace them on the railroad.

If horses had been aware of current events, they would have started to worry when Frenchman Nicolas Cugnot invented the first self-propelled steam vehicle in 1769. Richard Trevithick, an Englishman, used this new technology to build his steam locomotive, the Puffing Devil, in 1801. He took some friends for a short ride, but the Puffing

A reproduction of Trevithick's Puffing Devil.

Devil couldn't go far. Three years later, Samuel Homfray, the owner of Penydarren Ironworks in Merhyr Tydfil, Wales, financed Trevithick to build an engine to replace horse-drawn wagons on the ironworks' railroad. Trevithick's new locomotive pulled five wagons with 10 tons of iron and 70 passengers on iron rails for 9 miles from the ironworks to the Merhyr-Cardiff Canal. The Penydarren locomotive was the first steam engine to run on rails; unfortunately, it broke them. Homfray cut the funding and abandoned the project. Other inventors recognized Trevithick's contribution to railroads, earning him a place in history, but his locomotives were not financially successful. He died broke in 1833.[31]

Near the famous coal mining town of Newcastle, England, a boy named George Stephenson watched horses pull coal carts on wooden tracks. As a teenager in the 1790s, he worked with his father in the Dewly Colliery (a coal mining operation), where George learned about engines.

In 1814, Stephenson built a locomotive he called the *Blutcher* that pulled 30 tons uphill at 4 miles per hour for the Killingworth Colliery. In 1819, the colliery bosses had Stephenson build an 8-mile railroad, the first to use locomotives instead of animals. Two years later, Parliament authorized a horse-drawn railway to be built between collieries in Darlington and Stockton, England. Stephenson told the Stockton & Darlington Railway Company that his Blutcher locomotive was "worth 50 horses." When Edward Pease, the railway

Stevenson's locomotive, Blutcher, was worth 50 horses.

owner, saw what the Blutcher could do, horses were out, locomotives were in. Stephenson became the chief engineer for Stockton & Darlington.

Pease, Stephenson, and Stephenson's son Robert founded Robert Stephenson & Company, the first company to make locomotives, in 1823.[32]

The first American railroad, the Baltimore & Ohio (the B&O), started in 1830. An early account of a ride on the B&O said, "You will mount a car, something like a stage, and then you will be drawn along by two horses, at the rate of 12 miles an hour."[33] The B&O's owners knew of England's progress with locomotives, but wondered if the new technology would work on American railroads.

In the summer of 1830, Peter Cooper,‡ an inventor from New York, demonstrated his locomotive *Tom Thumb* on the B&O. Tom Thumb carried a car with B&O directors and their friends for a round trip of 26 miles at an average speed of 15 miles per hour. When the train reached the speed of 18 miles per hour, some of the men wrote their names in notebooks to prove they could write while going so fast.

Horses didn't give up easily. Soon after Tom Thumb's historic run, the Stockton & Stokes Stagecoach Company arrived with a gray horse and challenged Tom Thumb to a race—the locomotive on one track, the horse-drawn car on the second track. The engine and the horse started at the same time. At first, the horse had the advantage, but once the engine picked up speed it raced past the horse. The race seemed won for Tom Thumb, but the engine malfunctioned and slowed down. Cooper fixed the problem and got the engine back up to speed, but the horse had already passed and won the race.[34]

In spite of the horse's win that day, railroad men realized the speed, power, and reliability of locomotives would continue to improve, making them the transportation of choice for the future.

---

‡   Peter Cooper also founded the Cooper Union for Advancement of Science and Art and invented the gelatin dessert that became JELL-O®

"All Aboard!"

At the train station, everyone recognized the man with striped hat, he was the engineer. They knew the man looking at his watch and calling, "All Aboard!" was the conductor. These figures are so iconic, even we modern car-driving people recognize them.

Pat Moran, a colorful fellow the Louisville *Courier-Journal* described as "short tempered, cussing, and cocky," was the Mammoth Cave Railroad engineer for many years.

To drive the locomotive, Pat maneuvered the Johnson bar, a vertical lever that controls the amount of steam driving the pistons that powers the wheels, sort of like a manual transmission gear shift in a car. This took skill; to change the direction of the pistons and

Engineer Pat Moran, conductor Robert Hatcher, and fireman B.H. Age worked together to keep the train running.

put the engine in reverse, the engineer had to move the Johnson bar at exactly the right time. If he moved it at the wrong time, too much steam could escape, causing the engine to stall.

Engineers needed a watchful eye. Pat had to navigate the curves and hills and be prepared for unexpected obstacles, like an occasional cow or other animal on the track. One day while driving *Hercules*, Pat saw a mule standing stubbornly on the track. The engineer blew the whistle and rang the bell. Unwilling to budge, the mule kicked out the locomotive's headlight. *Hercules* was repaired, the mule was less fortunate.

Soapy rails could also stall the train. Local kids thought this was great fun. When it happened, passengers sometimes had to get out and push, much to the delight of the pranksters who took the time to soap up the rails.

When the engineer saw soap (or water, ice, wet leaves, or other slippery things) on the rails, he moved a lever to release sand onto the tracks for traction. The sand, stored in a dome on the boiler, ran through a tube that opened in front of the wheels.

Some boys went a step beyond soap and laid nails on the tracks. This could derail the train, but most kids just wanted the nails to be flattened into what they called "breast-pins." "Every boy had one," said Jewell Furlong, who grew up near Mammoth Cave.[35]

J.B. Whitney, the conductor, was in charge of the train and crew. Assisted by his son in the busy season, Whitney collected passengers' tickets and saw to their needs. Robert Hatcher, George James, and B.F. Lloyd also conducted.[36, 37, 38, 39, 40] Elbert Hubbard, a popular writer, talked with one of them in 1907:

> The conductor—there is only one on the road—came for my fare and said, "two dollars, please!" I handed out the money.
> "Well, say it!" he exclaimed.
> "Say what?" I asked.
> "What is in your head. Out with it!"
> "What do you want me to say or do?" I asked.
> "Why kick, protest, rail, or balk at being charged two dollars for riding 9 miles and back."
> "I never kick on any railroad that has less than 10 miles of mileage," I said.[41]

The fireman was less visible than the engineer or conductor, but equally important. A railroad fireman's job was not to put fires out, but to keep them burning. Pete Charlet, the M.C.R.R. fireman, shoveled coal into the locomotive's firebox to heat the boiler to make steam. The small platform the fireman stood on didn't leave much room to move, making a hot, back-breaking job even tougher. How much coal he shoveled depended on how much power the engine needed to go up or down hills, speed up or slow down. Virgil Wood, B.H. Age, and Landis Charlet also worked as firemen and engineers on the Mammoth Cave Railroad.

The M.C.R.R. carried mostly passengers and had no freight cars, but the train occasionally dropped off farm tools, spools of thread, and other goods to the Mammoth Cave Hotel and families who lived along the railroad. The railroad also delivered mail to Mammoth Cave.[42]

Typically, the train made three round-trips a day, although sometimes large groups, such as school field trips, warranted extra runs. Two engines usually hibernated in the winter when tourism waned.[43]

Old accounts boast of a perfect safety record for the M.C.R.R., but there may have been one death on the little railroad. A train struck and killed local wagon maker and blacksmith Aaron Tibbs as he walked on the tracks near Glasgow Junction in the 1890s. Years of hammering away at the anvil damaged Tibbs' hearing, leading his great-grandson to believe Tibbs was killed by a quiet dummy engine instead of a larger, noisier L&N train.[44]

Nine Miles to Mammoth Cave

The Passengers

In *A Trip Through Mammoth Cave*, David Tarbell wrote about his train ride to the cave in 1900:

> "Pay two more and ask for a deed of the road," suggested a passenger across the aisle, a Chicago man with a breezy, sporty look. Meanwhile an individual with a blond mustache and determined air stood there, holding out his hand and repeating,
> "Two dollars, if you please!"
> "Yes, but you don't seem to understand. I am not conducting an orphans' excursion, nor do I want to go across the state, or to any place else than Mammoth Cave, which is only 8 miles and a half from here, and ..."
> "Two dollars!"
> "He'll raise you another dollar in a minute if you don't cough quick," remarked the Chicago man.

Tarbell and the Chicago man feared prices at the cave would be as steep as the cost of the train ticket, but Tarbell was pleased to learn that a hotel room, a cave tour, and "more souvenirs—stalactites, stalagmites, and the like than he can comfortably carry," each cost about $2.00, a price he thought reasonable.[45] But don't expect to buy souvenir stalactites at any price today; it's illegal to sell cave formations.

By World War I, tickets cost less, but passengers weren't always satisfied. Around 1917, John H. Slater wrote in a letter:

> The Mammoth Cave Railroad is some railroad and they have more nerve than the Cadiz Railroad. For a distance of 9 miles the fare is $1.00 plus war tax. And the speed is almost as fast as one can walk while the road bed is fierce. Cadiz "slinky" is like riding on a cloud in comparison."[46]

Nine Miles to Mammoth Cave

The Cadiz Railroad connected the towns of Cadiz and Gracey, Kentucky, 8 miles apart. It is said that the Cadiz Railroad could not officially be called a railroad unless it had it least 10 miles of track, so the builders added 2 extra miles of curves, causing the "slinky" effect.

Many early 20th century travelers found the slow, rough Mammoth Cave train ride old fashioned. In his book *Romantic America*, Robert Haven Schauffler wrote in 1913:

> The privately owned line of railway from Glasgow Junction to the cave is like a quaint toy ... . It was propelled, with a scarcely perceptible motion, by a genial little open-faced engine of the kind one may see on those old print handkerchiefs designed in the stirring days when locomotives were more novel than biplanes are now.[47]

Even Mammoth Cave Railroad employees joked about the train. Elbert Hubbard, a popular turn-of-the-century writer, wrote in 1907:

> "You notice," said the conductor, "that we have our cowcatcher on the rear end, so as to keep the cows out of the ladies' coach." He then explained, "Why a bull got after us last week and would have ketched us, too, if we hadn't been on the down grade."[48]

Hubbard also revealed a common racial attitude of the era. He wrote, "I was interested in seeing a Kaffir cutting the grass between streaks of rust" on the railroad tracks. Seldom heard today, "Kaffir," a derogatory term for a black person, reflects a common view of black people in Hubbard's day. In the 1800s and early 1900s, few black people could afford to go to vacation destinations like Mammoth Cave. Many who visited the cave were servants traveling with white employers. Black travelers were segregated from white travelers on the train, cave tours, and at the Mammoth Cave Hotel. At first, black passengers rode in the baggage area of the combination coaches. In 1892, a Jim Crow law§ called for separate compartments for black

---

§   Reconstruction after the Civil War encouraged equal rights for blacks. People against equal treatment responded by creating Jim Crow laws in the late 1800s to enforce the unequal separation of blacks (and other minorities) from whites.

people on trains, so the railroad put a partition up to separate the last two seats from the rest of the coach.[49]

Segregation on trains and elsewhere often surprised Europeans visiting the South. On a trip to Mammoth Cave in 1888, British traveler Alfred Smedley wrote about the L&N depot in Louisville:

> We were surprised to see the following notice over one of the doors on the platform, "Colored Passengers Waiting Room," and were still more surprised to learn that it was generally complied with by the Negroes. We also found that on this Railway, the Negros had cars to themselves. It is the first time we have seen anything of the kind in passing through the states and we have traveled nearly 1,000 miles since landing in New York.
>
> ... Speaking with some of them about it, we asked them why they did not pull the notice board down at the Railway Station? They answered that it ought to be pulled down but none of them cared to take the responsibility of such a step. ... We informed them that if we lived there we would have the notice board down in less than a fortnight."[50]

Nine Miles to Mammoth Cave

Where Are We Going?

Nowadays, as you drive to Mammoth Cave from Park City (Glasgow Junction), you'll see a lot of trees, some white-tailed deer, and an occasional wild turkey. In the old days, Mammoth Cave Railroad passengers gazed out their windows at cattle grazing in pastures, kids playing in yards, dogs lounging on front porches, and signs enticing them to visit show caves other than Mammoth. The train stopped at those caves and some neighborhoods on its way to its main destination.

Train Stops	Miles from Glasgow Junction
Diamond Caverns	1.5
Chaumont Post Office	2
Grand Avenue Cave (A spur 1½ miles off the main line.)	3
Union City	2.5
Proctor's Hotel	3
Sloans Crossing	4
Ganter's Hotel	7.5
Mammoth Cave	8.7[51]

Diamond Caverns

According to legend, a slave (we don't know his name) belonging to Jessie Coats discovered a magnificent cave on his master's land on July 14, 1859. Stalactites dripping from the ceiling like limestone icicles, draperies of stone, and columns worthy of a coliseum (but no diamonds) prompted Coats to open the cave for tours that same year.[52] According to *Guide Book for the Diamond Cave* written in

The first stop on the Mammoth Cave Railroad, Diamond Caverns is still popular with cave visitors today.

1870, a wedding party climbed in on ladders for the first tour. The guide book lured travelers by boasting "Diamond Cave is the most beautiful Cave in America" and that "the grandeur, beauty, and sublimity of the Diamond Cave far surpass anything ever dreamed of in our philosophy ... ."[53]

When the M.C.R.R. opened in 1886, Seth Shackleford, whose relatives had worked at Mammoth Cave, owned Diamond Caverns.[54] You can still see privately owned Diamond Caverns, which is the only show cave other than Mammoth still open for tours along the M.C.R.R. route. Today you'll descend into the cave on stairs instead of ladders.

Chaumont Post Office

Chaumont, located at what is now the park boundary, had no show caves or other tourist attractions, but the train stopped there to deliver mail. A traveler around 1910 wrote:

> When I expressed regret at having forgotten to stop at the post-office, the conductor, a young lad in plain clothes obligingly said he would fix that all right. He opened the front door and called to the engineer. We stopped. The conductor sauntered across the road and in a few minutes strolled back with a bundle of

Where are we Going?

Grand Avenue Cave and Procter's Cave

These Two Celebrated Caves are now Open to Visitors

GRAND AVENUE is situated three miles from the Louisville and Nashville Railroad, at Glasgow Junction, and within 1,100 yards of the depot on Cave Railroad.

PROCTER'S CAVE is situated five miles from the Junction, and four hundred yards from depot on Cave Railroad.

Stop-over privileges on all regular trains from Glasgow Junction to Mammoth Cave, without payment of additional fare, either going or coming, to visit one or both of these Caves, and tickets can be procured at Glasgow Junction to visit one or both Grand Avenue and Procter's Caves at prorata rates for the distance.

CAVE FEE: $1 AT EACH CAVE.

The grounds and buildings at Grand Avenue have been put in perfect order, and everything is neat and clean. A small but comfortable dining room is attached to the buildings, and a first class Lunch and Coffee Stand will be kept for the accommodation of visitors. Charges low and reasonable and nothing charged for what you do not get. Rates charged will be $1.25 per day or 40 cents for single meal. I intend to give satisfaction or make no charge.

Parties can visit Grand Avenue from Glasgow Junction and return, including railroad fare, conveyance from depot and return, and Cave fee, for $2.25; or they can visit both Grand Avenue and Procter's, the round trip, for $4.00.

Parties arriving at Glasgow Junction on the night or early morning trains will find there good hotel accommodations, at reasonable rates. They can take the 7 o'clock morning train, visit Grand Avenue and Procter's Cave and return to the Junction in time for the evening or night trains.

If you want to see a Cave with the

Largest, Grandest and Most Beautiful Avenue

of any Cave in America, then come and see the Grand Avenue. If you want to see the most magnificent dome in the world, then come and view Echo Dome in Echo Avenue, with its lofty columns, fluted and garnished walls, extending 170 feet over head; and listen to the charming echo, answering back to your voice from the secret chambers of this mighty and vast Cave. If you want to see a Stalagmite 90 feet high, 40 feet in diameter, at the side of which is suspended a cluster of Stalactites 20 feet long, in the shape of scrolls and curtains; then come and see them at the summit of the Rocky Mountains. This vast Stalagmite in shape resembles the dome upon the capitol at Washington, and is more imposing. If you want to see a crescent or half dome of most exquisite shape and beauty and over 100 feet high, then come and see it in Lee's Avenue. If you want to see a column of pure alabaster over 20 feet in height, extending from the floor to the ceiling of the Cave, then come and see it in Echo Avenue. If you want to see grape clusters, swarms of bees, pine apples and a thousand other exquisitely shaped formations of delicate Stalactites, then come and see them for miles in the Main and Echo Avenues. If you want to see the Hall of Stalagamite Pillows and statues of unrivaled beauty, then come and see them in Briggs' Avenue. If you want to see a Cave with the most beautiful Stalactites and Stalagmite formations to be seen in any Cave in America, then come and see them in Procter's Cave and if not satisfied we will charge no Cave fee

Guides' Manuals can be procured at Glasgow Junction descriptive of these Caves at Cave Exchange, opposite depot

L. J. PROCTER.

This 1889 ad touted "a Stalagmite 90 feet high" at Grand Avenue Cave – an exaggeration, but it attracted customers.

my letters, which, in the leisurely Southern fashion, had lingered there a few days of recuperation in their exhausting pilgrimage to the Mammoth Cave Hotel.[55]

BONUS TRIVIA! Though Chaumont had no attractions in the days of the railroad and has none today, in the 1970s and 1980s it had a small theme park called Wondering Woods, which featured faux 1800s buildings, live music, and crafts. A scene from the movie Big Business (1988) starring Bette Midler and Lily Tomlin was filmed there. Wondering Woods closed in the 1980s. The land is now part of Mammoth Cave National Park.

Grand Avenue Cave

Mammoth Cave's and Diamond Caverns' success stories encouraged local entrepreneurs to take advantage of travelers' appetites for the underground by developing other show caves. Larkin J. Proctor, his wife Mary, and his brother George (who also helped commercialize Diamond Caverns) bought Grand Avenue Cave in 1876 for $700 and opened it for tours.[56] Larkin Proctor played a big role in local tourism and the Mammoth Cave Railroad. Before the railroad opened, Proctor owned a stagecoach line between Glasgow Junction and Mammoth Cave. He helped found the M.C.R.R., leased Mammoth Cave from 1856 to 1861 and from 1866 to 1871,[57] and owned Grand Avenue Cave, Proctor Cave, and Proctor's Hotel. He used his influence to get a mile and a half long spur to run from the main M.C.R.R. line to Grand Avenue Cave.

Discovered in the 1790s, Grand Avenue Cave was originally called Wrights Cave, after W.W. Wright, an early cave explorer, and Pit Cave, for several treacherous pits. Robert Mongomery Bird's 1838 book *Peter Pilgrim: or A Rambler's Recollections*, includes a story of Wright and a miner exploring the cave's saltpeter mining potential in the early 1800s

> But by and by, having consumed much time in rambling about, they discovered that by some extraordinary oversight, they had left their store of candles at the mouth of the cave, having brought in with them only those they carried in their hands, which were now burning low. The horrors of their situation at once flashed on their minds; they were at a great distance from the entrance, which there was little hope they could reach with what remained of their

candles, and the terrible pits were directly on their path.[58]

Crawling toward what they hoped was the entrance, the men tossed rocks in front of them, trying to detect the pits. In spite of their caution, Wright fell down a 50-foot pit and died. Or so the story goes. W.W. Wright wrote his name on the cave wall in 1853, presumably very much alive.¶

Proctor's customers saw the huge pits as part of the fun and adventure of a cave trip. Proctor's carpenter, Thomas E. Lee, built several long, scary-looking ladders that descend into the pits. The ladders' name, the bonzai ladders, suits them. Bonzai is Japanese for an attack with no concern for your own death or injury, a fitting attitude for someone climbing these ladders. Twentieth-century cave explorers probably named them; few Americans knew the term bonzai prior to World War II.

Lee also explored caves. While exploring nearby Salts Cave, he and his companions, J.L. Lee and W.D. Cutliff, found a naturally preserved prehistoric American Indian mummy, a 9-year-old child. Originally called Little Alice, a closer look in the 20th century revealed that Alice was really Al. Proctor displayed the mummy in Grand Avenue Cave and claimed Lee had found it there. Stories of a lost Indian maiden fleeing from her lover, or a settler's daughter hiding in the cave from "a blood thirsty savage,"[59] lured curious travelers to Grand Avenue Cave even after Proctor no longer owned the mummy.

Some people thought if the cave atmosphere preserved a mummy, it could preserve food. People in cave country often used cold cave air or water to store perishable food by building spring houses over springs exiting caves to take advantage of water that stayed cold year round regardless of the temperature above ground. An article in the March 28, 1896, edition of the Louisville *Courier-Journal* claimed Mammoth Cave Railroad president Colonel R.H. Lacey kept eggs in Grand Avenue Cave for a year and that citrus fruits had been successfully stored for months (pieces of orange crates are still in the cave). Proctor had wooden tracks laid to transport food into the cave, but for unknown reasons he eventually abandoned the plan to use

---

¶ Bird's story does not include Wright's first name, so the man who fell down the pit may have been a different Wright.

A 21st century caver ascending a bonsai ladder in Grand Avenue Cave. Photo by Rick Olson.

the cave for food storage.[60]

In May of 1889, Proctor advertised a package deal that included M.C.R.R. fare, transportation from the Chaumont depot to Grand Avenue Cave (the spur hadn't opened yet), and a cave tour for $2.25. He threw in a tour of Proctor Cave down the road for an extra $1.75.

Hungry travelers could get meals for the whole day at the "first-class Lunch and Coffee Stand" for $1.25; the special deal for meals was no bargain; one meal cost only 40 cents.[61]

Grand Avenue Cave, A Description in Detail of One of America's Greatest Natural Wonders, a book published in 1892, states on the cover that Grand Avenue Cave is "on the line of Mammoth Cave Railroad." Like all show cave guide books, it makes sure the reader knew this cave is superior to all others, especially that big cave at the end of the rail line. It says:

> Mammoth Cave has for years been a popular resort for lovers of subterranean grandeurs, but recently the tide of visitors has been turned toward Grand Avenue Cave, whose rare and varied attractions, even while it has not yet been thoroughly explored, make it a formidable rival of its distinguished neighbor, and which when all of its devious windings have been traced to their gloomy limits, will certainly surpass, in the number, variety, sublimity, and beauty of its attractions, all the other great caverns of the world.[62]

Proctor sold the cave to railroad president R.H. Lacy in 1891. Automobile traffic and lack of visitors to Grand Avenue Cave eventually caused the spur to the cave to fall into disuse and the tracks were removed by the 1920s. In 1926, the M.C.R.R. considered replacing the rails so it could keep its right-of-way, but it wasn't worth the cost and never happened.[63]

Today Grand Avenue Cave is called Long Cave.

Union City

Locals took the train to Union City to buy food and household goods at John Newton "Newt" France's country store.

In the 1920s, the crossroads at Union City became a decision point for tourists in automobiles; they had to choose whether to take the road to the Historic Entrance owned by the Mammoth Cave Estate, or drive to the separately owned New Entrance to Mammoth Cave that opened in 1921. Railroad passengers were bound for the Historic Entrance. Today, park visitors enjoy trips into both parts of the cave.

Nine Miles to Mammoth Cave

Passengers could ride the train to Newt France's country store in Union City. The road leading to the New Entrance of Mammoth Cave is in the background.

Proctor's Hotel and Cave

If travelers didn't get off the train and spend money at his Grand Avenue Cave, Proctor hoped to get their business down the line at Proctors Cave and Proctor's Hotel.

According to Helen F. Randolph's 1924 book *Mammoth Cave and the Cave Region of Kentucky*, an escaped slave returning to his master's home during the Civil War discovered Proctors Cave. Randolph, who had a romantic view of slavery, wrote that Jonathan Doyle (or Doyel) ran away from his master, a Baptist preacher. Doyle cooked for the Union Army, but didn't like army food, so he "turned his face toward Mammoth Cave, seeking forgiveness and pork-chops." As Doyle neared his master's house he worried that his master would be angry with him, so he camped in the woods until he found the master's children to ask about his status; they assured him he would be welcomed back.

In the woods, Doyle felt a breeze coming from a crack in a rock. Having grown up in cave country, he knew breezes blowing from rocks came from caves, so he began to dig out an entrance. He marked his discovery and headed home.

After returning to his master's house, Doyle continued to explore the cave, which eventually Proctor bought and opened for tours. After the Civil War, Doyle worked at the cave as a guide.[64]

Randolph's story implies Doyle was AWOL and ran back to slavery,

Where are we Going?

Jonathan Doyle, a slave and Civil War soldier, discovered Proctor Cave.

but pension records show that Doyle enlisted in the U.S. Cavalry on September 24, 1864, and was discharged as disabled with chronic rheumatism on October 10, 1865, a free man, six months after the war ended. He received a military pension until he died in 1910.[65, 66]

Although Proctor advertised that his Grand Avenue Cave surpassed "all other great caverns of the world," he touted Proctors Cave as "unrivaled by any cave in America for the beauty and variety of its stalactite and stalagmite formations."

Guests could stay at Proctor's "new, neat, and commodious Hotel" by the cave for $2.00 a day.[67, 68]

Proctor lived for a while near Grand Avenue Cave, then moved to the Proctor Hotel, where he died in 1895. His grandson James Proctor sold Proctors Cave and the hotel to the L&N Railroad in 1901. L&N eventually donated the land to Mammoth Cave National Park.[69]

In the days of the railroad, Proctor (and everyone else) thought

Nine Miles to Mammoth Cave

Proctor's "new, neat, and commodious hotel."

his cave was separate from Mammoth Cave, but in 1979, cave explorers found a connection between the two.

Sloans Crossing

The roads to Mammoth Cave, Glasgow Junction, and Brownsville intersect at Sloans Crossing. Mostly locals used this stop because it had no attractions. But some communities that lacked show caves and hotels had other services for tourists. One passenger bound for Mammoth Cave commented on a stop along the way:

> Now and again we would pause for friendly visits at crossroad haunts of cracker-box clubs, their walls propped up by leaning timbers, and with shaggy colts restive outside."[70]

Today, a pond, a scenic trail, and picnic tables make Sloans Crossing a popular place for picnics and leisurely strolls.

Ganter's Hotel

Henry C. Ganter managed the Mammoth Cave Hotel from the 1860s until 1902 and published many of the cave's first postcards, which are popular with collectors. He also operated his own hotel, probably after leaving his position at the Mammoth Cave Hotel. Ganter's Hotel may not have had a lot of business; I've seen no brochures or travelers' accounts of the hotel, but the train stopped there.

Henry C. Ganter managed the Mammoth Cave Hotel and operated Ganter's Hotel.

Mammoth Cave

Travelers enjoyed the caves, hotels, and watering holes along the railroad, but their ultimate destination was at the end of the track.

Big groups meant big money for Mammoth Cave and the railroad. The groups could arrange special train trips. The Knights of Pythias, a fraternal organization promoting peace and friendship, held their Encampment and Biennial Conclave (translation: secret meeting held every two years) in Louisville in August of 1904. The L&N Railroad provided transportation for the event and printed

Ganter's Hotel.

brochures advertising side trips from the encampment to Mammoth Cave, the Saint Louis World's Fair, Cumberland Gap, Nashville, and other sites. The brochure touted the cave as "The greatest cavern in the world, and one of America's Great Natural Wonders. An explored region of 200 miles under ground," although less than 30 miles had been explored at the time.** The $4.00 fare covered two cave tours, passage on the L&N train, and "a picturesque mountain railroad," the M.C.R.R. (The L&N's lease on the M.C.R.R. had expired, but the railroads still cooperated).[71] The Knights built a stone monument commemorating their visit in Mammoth Cave's Gothic Avenue, where it still stands today.

The Mammoth Cave Estate (which owned the cave and hotel), the L&N, and M.C.R.R. sponsored the Louisville Public School Children's Day at Mammoth Cave on December 7, 1912. Children attending the Louisville White Graded Schools could buy a $1.65

** Cave guides and writers have touted Mammoth Cave as the longest cave in the world since it first became a tourist attraction. This wildly exaggerated claim became true in 1972 when a Cave Research Foundation survey team found a passage linking Mammoth Cave to Flint Ridge Cave, bringing the length of the cave to 144 miles. As of 2011, explorers have discovered and mapped 390 miles.

Where are we Going?

Members of the Knights of Pythias rode the train to Mammoth Cave from their Biennial Conclave in Louisville.

train ticket and get a free ticket to the cave. The invitation did not include minority students: schools, railroads, and cave tours were all segregated. Adults accompanying students paid $3.25 for the train and $1.00 (half price) for the cave trip. Children and parents could also buy a ticket to a special underground dinner in the cave's Audubon Avenue, specially decorated for Christmas. These extra costs made the "free" cave trip quite profitable for both Mammoth Cave and the railroads.[72]

Students at Potter College, a ladies' college (now part of Western Kentucky University) in Bowling Green, eagerly anticipated a train

45

trip to Mammoth Cave every year. In 1908, the student paper, *The Green and Gold*, reported:

> "Twenty-three for Mammoth Cave! Skiddoo!" This is what the conductor shouted as 23 Potter girls and their chaperones boarded the train Friday, October 23rd, for the cave. Soon Glasgow Junction was reached; here we changed cars and waited for the other train about an hour. We were not idle during that hour, some wrote postals or took Kodak pictures and all were eating candy, chestnuts, or anything we could get to eat.
>
> When the queer little train came in for Mammoth Cave, we could not get on fast enough, as all were eager to get to our journey's end.

Well prepared for the cave tour, the girls' chaperone carried a bottle of "Kentucky Moonshine" in case a student should "fall by the wayside."[73]

Doing Business

Mammoth Cave drew travelers to the area and spurred the creation of the Mammoth Cave Railroad, but the owners of other show caves along the route didn't want to be ignored, which caused a disagreement about the railroad's name. Proctor wanted to call it the Glasgow Junction, Diamond Cave, Proctor Cave, and Mammoth Cave Railroad Company. An early charter from the General Assembly of the Commonwealth of Kentucky authorizing the building of the railroad used this name,[74] but it didn't last long. In July of 1885, 16 months before the train's first run, the managers of the railroad and Mammoth Cave Estate met at the Mammoth Cave Hotel and agreed to change the railroad's name to the Mammoth Cave Railroad Company.[75]

Proctor did not give up easily; he took the Mammoth Cave Railroad Company to court in 1894 in an attempt to change the railroad's name to Kentucky Cave Railroad Company.[76] As one of the founders of M.C.R.R. and a successful businessman, Proctor had influence, and the name he suggested was fairer to other caves on the line. But Mammoth Cave Estate also had clout and, more important to the railroad owners, name recognition, so the name Mammoth Cave Railroad stuck.

In a legal agreement, Proctor dropped the law suit and transferred his rights in the original railroad charter to the Mammoth Cave Railroad. As part of the deal, the railroad promised that ticket agents would inform passengers of the stop at Proctors Cave, the conductor would announce the name when the train stopped there, rail tickets to Proctors Cave would cost the same per mile as those to Mammoth Cave, Proctor's employees would get a discount on the train, and Proctor could hand out ads for his businesses on the trains.[77]

Although the L&N Railroad's lease on the Mammoth Cave Railroad didn't expire until 1911, L&N sold the M.C.R.R. under foreclosure on March 17, 1898, and in 1900 transferred it to a

This $1,000 bond in the Mammoth Cave Railroad Company promised the investor six percent interest.

reorganized company representing original stockholders. The newly independent Mammoth Cave Railroad issued $16,000 in stock and $30,000 in bonds. Stockholders elected R.H. Lacey, the railroad's secretary and one of its founders, as the new president and secretary for a salary of $5.00 a year.

Railroad workers moved the turnout to direct the train onto a specific fork in the track.

After the sale, the two railroads continued to cooperate. In 1906, L&N charged the M.C.R.R. $5.02 a year to use the L&N turnout (a mechanism that directs trains onto another track) and in 1916, $100 a year to use the L&N west passing track in Glasgow Junction.

Here is how much money the Mammoth Cave Railroad made from 1888 to 1908. Not all the numbers are available for every year.

Nine Miles to Mammoth Cave

Year	Freight	Passengers	Express	Mail	Gross Income	Expenses	Net Income
1888–1989	$1,374.40	$8,004.52	$24.75	$363.80	$9,767.47	$7,806	$1,961.47
1889–1890	$1,453.45	$8,718.82	$50.50	$357.13	$10,579.90	$8,153	$2,426.90
1890–1891					$11,417	$8,525	$2,892
1891–1892	$1,318.28	$8,022.74	$95.65	$367.57	$9,804.24	$8,371.24	$1,433
1982–1893					$8,956	$8,385	$571
1893–1894					$7,062	$8,832	($1,770)*
1894–1895					$5,835	$8,753	($2,918)*
1897					$4,315	$3,032	$1,283
1899					$7,640	$7,092	$548
1900					$5,923		
1901					$7,695	$5,288	$2,407
1907					$9,806	$9,428	$378
1908					$10,436	$9,761	$675

*Years in deficit[78]

From 1893 to 1895, the M.C.R.R. lost money, and even in profitable years didn't make much (although no one expected the little railroad to make much).

On his 1907 visit to the cave, popular writer Elbert Hubbard heard about the railroad's financial trouble. He wrote in his magazine *The Philistine*:

> "The Mammoth Cave Railroad belongs to the Mammoth Cave estate, and the estate is so poor and the heirs so greedy that the engineer told me he had hard work to get grease for his cylinders."[79]

Hubbard was mistaken about ownership, Mammoth Cave Estate owned Mammoth Cave and the hotel, but not the railroad.

By 1910, the railroad owed $8,216. The directors issued 30, $1,000 bonds at 6% yearly interest to pay the debt and raise money for extra expenses.

The railroad soon spent the money raised through the bonds. The M.C.R.R. directors wanted the railroad spiffed up for the arrival of The Women's Club, which held its yearly meeting at Mammoth Cave in 1912. The club strongly supported making Mammoth Cave a national park (which happened in 1941). The directors also wanted the park, believing it would boost the railroad's business, so they spent $4,000 of the money from the bonds to improve the track and equipment.

The next year, they improved the track again to allow L&N sleeping cars to run to the cave,[80] although passengers would have had time only for a short nap. Sleeping cars never ran on the tracks.

Hoping for a future with lots of eager passengers riding to a newly created Mammoth Cave National Park, the directors overhauled the little railroad, but it was doomed. In June of 1903, an automobile club left Chicago with 20 motorcars bound for Mammoth Cave.[81]

A Railroad Retires

When the first automobiles arrived at Mammoth Cave, only the rich could afford cars, but with the introduction of the Ford Model T in 1909, cars became more affordable and common on America's roads, including the roads to Mammoth Cave.

Fewer cave visitors arrived by train. What little money the M.C.R.R. took in went to pay interest on bonds. The railroad owed money and the bright future the directors hoped for dimmed with each arriving automobile. On February 1, 1928, M.C.R.R.'s president, L.P. Lacey (the railroad's late president E.H. Lacey's widow) sold the railroad, stocks, and bonds to a company from Michigan for $84,000.

The new company's president, F.L. Gallup, and secretary-treasurer Lee Thompson planned on extending the tracks to asphalt deposits they owned in Edmonson County, where Hercules and his cohorts would be demoted to hauling asphalt. The asphalt deposits proved unprofitable, the tracks were never extended, and the Michiganders lost about $200,000 on the asphalt/railroad scheme.

The directors cut costs by retiring Hercules and the other dummy engines—probably the last ones in the United States. The last train ran to the cave on February 28, 1929.

People loved Hercules even though the engine was old fashioned and obsolete. The May 21, 1929, edition of the Bowling Green *Daily News* announced,

> Noted "Hercules" No More To Make Picturesque Cave Trip. Although a misfit in the realm of transportation and the butt of many deserved jokes, it still was probably the most famous locomotive in America and is said to have been photographed more times than any other steam engine in existence.[82]

The Mammoth Cave Railroad still had a contract to carry the mail to Mammoth Cave for $80 a month. The day after the train

When the train retired, a bus fitted with railroad wheels carried the mail to Mammoth Cave for a while.

retired, a Ford bus mounted on train-like wheels that could run on the tracks carried the mail. The M.C.R.R. had experimented with railbuses in 1910, but they didn't work out. Desperate, the directors were willing to give the railbus another chance.[83] Small turntables were installed at each end of the track to turn the railbus around.[84]

L&N Railroad tried to help by cutting the rent on their west passing track in Glasgow Junction from $100 a year to $25, but cheaper rent and a bus on wheels couldn't save the M.C.R.R. In 1930, the railroad's gross income was $2,026.56, but it spent $2,926.99. On March 31, 1931, the Mammoth Cave National Park Association (MCNPA) bought the Mammoth Cave Railroad including property, right-of-way, equipment, stocks, and bonds for $5,000.[85] On June 8, the MCNPA voted to shut down the railroad. The railbus made its last run on August 31, 1931.[86]

A National Park and a New Life for a Train

Some people mistakenly believe national parks don't allow railroads and that the creation of Mammoth Cave National Park brought the end of the M.C.R.R. Actually, railroads strongly supported the parks ever since the creation of Yellowstone, the world's first national park in 1872. Parks attracted tourists, and tourists bought railroad tickets. L&N president Milton Smith was one of the first people to suggest making Mammoth Cave a national park around 1901.[87] In 1924, The L&N Railroad offered to donate 1,084 acres of land and 2,305 acres of cave rights to the park under the conditions that a national park with a suitable hotel, highway, and railroad be established in the cave region.[88] The national park, modern hotel, and highway all came about, but soon even railroad officials realized the Mammoth Cave Railroad had been replaced by private automobiles.

National Park visitors can still ride railroads at Grand Canyon and Cuyahoga Valley National Parks, Steamtown National Historic Site, and New River Gorge National River.

Although the L&N Railroad and others showed interest in making the cave a national park, the idea did not get far until the 1924 creation of the Mammoth Cave National Park Committee, which soon became the Mammoth Cave National Park Association. They charged a $1 membership fee to raise money to introduce a bill to make Mammoth Cave one of the first national parks in the East. Senator Richard P. Ernst of Kentucky introduced the bill to the Senate, and President Calvin Coolidge signed it in May of 1926.[89] The Mammoth Cave National Park Association purchased land (nearly 600 families lived in what is now the park), and the Civilian Conservation Corps†† built new roads, trails, and buildings, some of

---

†† The Civilian Conservation Corp, or CCC, worked in many national and state parks during the Great Depression in the 1930s. Park visitors across the country still enjoy CCC cabins, rest areas, and trails.

which visitors still use today. Mammoth Cave became a national park without government funding in 1936,⁹⁰ a national park with funding in 1941, and was formally dedicated in 1946.

When the railroad closed, the new mail delivery contract went to the Mammoth Cave Transportation Company that already made daily mail runs by bus from Cave City to the cave before the railbus stopped operating.⁹¹

A Mammoth Cave Transportation Company bus delivered mail to the cave via the road instead of the tracks.

When the train stopped running, people looked for new uses for the old equipment. In 1931, Mammoth Cave's superintendent M.L. Charlet (M.C.R.R. fireman Pete Charlet's brother) asked for a boiler from one of the dummy engines to use to provide steam for the laundry at the Mammoth Cave Hotel.⁹² Whether or not the boiler actually went from powering a locomotive to cleaning dirty laundry is lost to history.

Herman E. Drewing, a contractor from Tippecanoe City, Ohio, removed the rails as scrap.⁹³ Rumor has it, Italy bought the rails to use in Mussolini's 1935 invasion of Ethiopia; there's no documentation, but the timing fits.⁹⁴

In 1931, most people saw the M.C.R.R. equipment as junk, but Drewing saw it as history. He pointed out that the end of the railroad was the end of an era, and in a few years people would regard the engine and coach as artifacts. Convinced that they were worth saving, Charlet paid $25.61 to have a dummy engine and a car brought to the park for display. Forty years later, Drewing's daughter visited Mammoth Cave National Park, saw the train and reported to her father that park leaders took his advice.

Charlet wanted the famous engine Hercules for display, but Hercules had several flues cut out, making it unable to run from Glasgow Junction to the cave. Charlet had engine number 4 brought to the cave, painted the name Hercules on it, and displayed it as the more famous engine. For years, engine number 4 masqueraded as Hercules on the lawn near the Mammoth Cave Post Office and camp store until the engine was restored in 1999–2002. As part of the restoration, the crew sanded off the name Hercules and painted on a plain number 4, returning the engine to its 1931 identity.

But wait! Letters between Charlet and Mammoth Cave Estate trustee George E. Zubrod led some to think the engine's 1931 number may not have been its original name. The letters say that engine number 4 was originally Hercules and that the names had been changed years earlier.[95] Were the original names and numbers changed during an early 20th century paint job?

Even in the 1930s, Zubrod saw potential for confusion about which engine was which; he asked that the name Hercules be painted over before the broken engine was sent to the Bowling Green Normal School (now Western Kentucky University), where he promised to give it to manual training students.[96] The university has no record of the engine arriving.[97]

Is the engine on display the original Hercules, or has it always been engine number 4? A turn of the millennium restoration revealed the answer.

A Facelift for the New Millennium

The dummy engine and combination coach, listed on the National Register of Historic Places, has sat protected under a shed since the 1930s. In spite of this life of leisure, the train needs occasional work to keep it looking nice. In 1950, Park superintendent R. Taylor Hoskins authorized park employees to do a $1,000 fix-up project. In 1999, flatbed trucks hauled the engine, still called Hercules, and the coach to the Kentucky Railway Museum in New Haven for a $90,000 restoration by locomotive restoration professionals.

Because the Mammoth Cave Railroad ran for over 40 years and the equipment had gone through numerous repairs and paint jobs, the park had to decide which period to restore the train to. 1920s photos showed the train, so the park decided on that era.

Museum workers sandblasted the paint off the locomotive and

The engine on its way to the Kentucky Railway Museum for restoration. Photo compliments of the Kentucky Railway Museum.

found three layers of paint showing the number 4 in three different positions and styles from different eras. None said Hercules. The engine was always number 4 after all. The workers also found a 1953 penny painted to the wall, revealing the locomotive had been painted that year or after.[98]

Workers installed two new headlights, a new whistle, and two new builder's plates. The plates list the name and location of the manufacturer, when the engine was built, and a specific identification number—engine number 4's builder's number is 9442. Restoration workers marked the replacement parts so future train buffs and historians will know they are reproductions.

The builder's plate shows that engine #4 was built by Baldwin Locomotive Works in Philadelphia. Photo by Rick Olson

Workers painted, removed asbestos, repaired the roof, replaced glass, restored baggage compartment doors, did carpentry, welding, and other work.[99]

Still immobile but all spruced up, the train came home to a rebuilt display track in 2002.

The Kentucky Railway Museum's president, Mark Johnson, believes the restoration crew could have made the engine run, but with only a few yards of track, the train has nowhere to go.

Remembering the Mammoth Cave Railroad

Trains—especially steam locomotives—may seem old fashioned in the age of cars and airplanes, yet people love them. Children are fascinated by trains because they are big, powerful, and fast. The allure for their parents and grandparents may be nostalgia. Some people see railroads not just as part of the past, but of the future. One locomotive can pull a lot of cars, so trains move freight and people inexpensively and efficiently. Railroad use declined in the 20th century, but maybe freight and passenger trains will make a comeback in the 21st century.

Whether or not trains carry us into the future, the Mammoth Cave Railroad remains part of the past. Not much of it is left: a dummy engine, a coach, part of the railroad bed, some old photos of the train and passengers. Train lovers and history buffs visiting Mammoth Cave National Park can get a glimpse into the railroad's

If you had been a Mammoth Cave Railroad passenger in the late 1800s, you would have seen shops, farms, and homes, like the Beckner family's house near Union City.

*The author and what's left of the Proctor Hotel.
Photo by Rick Olson.*

history starting near the campground, where the train sits on what is left of the tracks. Today, the tracks go nowhere, but you can follow Hercules' path on the old railroad bed, now a bike and hike trail. Along the trail you will see berms (artificial ridges of earth or gravel) and road cuts that made the train ride through hilly country a little less hilly; but be prepared to go uphill, it's not all flat.

One hundred years ago, a person walking along the tracks would have seen and heard guests coming and going from Proctor's Hotel, people shopping and visiting at Newt France's store in Union City, and families working and playing in their yards. The din of human activity has been replaced with birds singing and squirrels chattering. You can walk by where Proctor's Hotel, France's store, and the home of a local family named Hawkins stood along the tracks; signs mark the locations. Nothing but stories remain of the hotel and store, although an old stone fireplace from Proctor's Hotel still stands as a remnant of a bygone era.

Want More Trains?

If reading about the Mammoth Cave Railroad got your locomotive going, don't miss these places to see trains and railroad artifacts in Kentucky.

The Kentucky Railway Museum. Located in the old railroad depot in New Haven, the museum has railroad artifacts, restored vintage trains, and a model train center. You can take a 90-minute train trip through Rolling Ford River Valley.

Bluegrass Scenic Railroad Museum. Attractions at this Versailles museum include a working telegraph and one-hour train ride through Kentucky's famous horse country.

The Historic Rail Park and Train Museum. Bowling Green's old L&N Depot has vintage railroad artifacts and equipment including a mail car, 1953 Pullman sleeper car, a 1949 Pullman diner, and a caboose.

Caldwell County Railroad Museum. This Princeton museum of railroad artifacts and memorabilia is open May through December.

Big South Fork Scenic Railway. You can board the train in Stearns for a 3-hour ride through Daniel Boone National Forest and Big South Fork National River and Recreation Area with a stop at the historic Blue Heron Coal Mining Camp.

My Old Kentucky Dinner Train. Passengers dine while riding in 1940s era dining cars pulled by a 1950s locomotive for a two hour ride from Bardstown.

Paducah Railroad Museum. Operated by the Paducah chapter of the National Railway Historical Society, the museum has equipment, memorabilia, and a model railroad room.

Lots of Thanks

This is a short book about a short railroad with a short history, but I had big help writing it. I owe a lot of gratitude to Normal Warnell, whose extensive collection of letters, court documents, brochures, and articles on the Mammoth Cave Rail Road was an enormous help. My National Park Service colleague, writer, and friend Nick Asher used his creative nonfiction writing expertise to help make this a better book. Others who provided information are Candice Leek, who gathered a lot of railroad documents; Coy Hanson, who told stories of his childhood shenanigans; Nicole Jackson, Curator at Penetanguishene Centennial Museum and Archives; Mick Woodcock, Chief Curator at Sharlot Hall Museum in Prescott, Arizona; Kate Burke, Fort Worden Area Parks Manager; Pamela Seighman, Curator at the Coal and Coke Heritage Center at Penn State; David Spence for telling the story of Aaron Tibbs; James Richey and Nancy Richey for telling me additional information about their great grandfather, Aaron Tibbs; Sally Beals for telling the story of her father Herman Drewing; Terry Langford, Mammoth Cave National Park Curator; Mark Johnson of the Kentucky Railway Museum for providing documents and photos of the restoration and for explaining all the components of the dummy locomotive to me; George Pritchard of the Federation of Old Cornwall Societies; The Kentucky Library at Western Kentucky University, where the world's most helpful librarians work; my friends and National Park Service colleagues Tres Seymour, Carol Pike, Darlene Owens, Steve Kistler, and John Yakel, who read the manuscript and gave me great advice; my sister-in-law, Debbie Stone, who gave me a non-Mammoth Caver's perspective; author Jennifer Bradbury who gave me great advice; and my husband, Rick Olson, who visited railroad museums with me, read the manuscript, and gave me feedback and lots of moral support.

Nine Miles to Mammoth Cave

Notes

1. Anonymous, 1816. "Mammoth Cave" *Thomas's Massachusetts Spy or Worcester Gazette. Worcester*, Massachusetts; July 17, 1816, p 4.
2. Blane, William N., 1824, *An Excursion Through The United States and Canada During the Years 1822–23*. London: Baldwin, Cradock, and Joy, pp 265–266.
3. Herr, Kincaid, 1964, *The Louisville and Nashville Railroad 1850–1963*. Louisville: Public Relation Department, L&N, pp 1–4, 25.
4. *Diamond Caverns Story*.
5. "Kentucky's Caves," *Courier-Journal*. August 17, 1877, p 5.
6. Sulzer, Elmer G., 1958, "The Mammoth Cave Railroad," *The Railway and Locomotive Historical Society, Bulletin No. 99*. Boston: Baker Library, Harvard Business School, p 31.
7. The *Glasgow Weekly Times*, June 14, 1886.
8. Letter from Thomas Andrew Chapman, March 25, 1977.
9. "Trail's End! The Mammoth Cave Railroad 1886-1931." *The L&N Employees Magazine*, May, 1932, p 6.
10. Herr, Kincaid, 1964, *The Louisville & Nashville Railroad*. Louisville: Public Relations Department, L&N, pp 103-104.
11. White, John H., 1998, "Dummy Tech," *Invention & Technology*, Spring, 1998, pp 34–37.
12. Letter from John H. White to Jim Carroll, May, 1991.
13. Furlong, Jewell W. "The End of the Line."
14. Sulzer, Elmer G., 1958, "The Mammoth Cave Railroad," *The Railway and Locomotive Historical Society, Bulletin No. 99*. Boston: Baker Library, Harvard Business School, p 34.
15. Personal communication with Coy Hanson, May, 2009.
16. Sulzer, Elmer G., 1958, "The Mammoth Cave Railroad," *The Railway and Locomotive Historical Society, Bulletin No. 99*. Boston: Baker Library, Harvard Business School, p 34.

17 Sulzer, Elmer G., 1958, "The Mammoth Cave Railroad," *The Railway and Locomotive Historical Society, Bulletin No. 99*. Boston: Baker Library, Harvard Business School, p 36.
18 "Trail's End! The Mammoth Cave Railroad 1886-1931," *The L&N Employees Magazine*, May, 1932, p 7.
19 Sulzer, Elmer G., 1958, "The Mammoth Cave Railroad," *The Railway and Locomotive Historical Society, Bulletin No. 99*. Boston: Baker Library, Harvard Business School, p 36.
20 *Ibid*, p 34.
21 Mammoth Cave Estate Fees ledger for 1886, Mammoth Cave National Park Curatorial.
22 "The Mammoth Cave Railroad," *The Washington Post*, October, 23, 1886, p 1.
23 *Hart County News*, Wednesday, November 24, 1886.
24 *Glasgow Weekly Times,* December 4, 1879, p 3.
25 Harlow, Alvin F. "Stagecoach Trip to Mammoth Cave in 1833."
26 Bridwell, Margaret M., 1952, *The Story of Mammoth Cave National Park Kentucky*.
27 Tissandier, Albert, 1885, "Six Months in the United States (1855 Journal)."
28 *Lebanon Weekly Standard*, October 8, 1873.
29 Joseph Warner Erwin's journal, 1852, http://www.brynmawr.edu.
30 Lewis, M.J.T., 1998, "Railways in the Greek and Roman World," Early Railways Conference, Durham, U.K.
31 "Biography of Richard Trevithick," http://www.spartacus.schoolnet.co.uk/RAtrevithick.htm.
32 Simkin, John. "George Stephenson: Biography," http://www.spartacus.schoolnet.co.uk/RAstephensonG.htm.
33 Hornung, Clarence P, 1959, *Wheels Across America*. New York; A.S Barnes & Co, p 90.
34 Latrobe, John H.B., 1974, *The Baltimore and Ohio Railroad*. Baltimore: Sun Printing Establishment.
35 Furlong, Jewell W. "End of the Line."
36 "Trail's End! The Mammoth Cave Railroad, 1886–1931," *The L&N Employees Magazine*, May, 1932, p 7.
37 *Hart County News*, Wednesday, November 10, 1886.
38 Sulzer, Elmer G., 1958, "The Mammoth Cave Railroad," *The Railroad and Locomotive Historical Society, Bulletin No. 99*.

Boston: Baker Library, Harvard Business School, p 35.
39 Asman, Larry, 1971, "Hercules and the Mammoth Cave Railroad," *Journal of Spelean History*. Vol 4, No. 3: Summer, 1971, p 56.
40 *The Glasgow Weekly Times*, September 4, 1895, p 3.
41 Hubbard, Elbert, 1907, *The Philistine*, Vol 25, June, 1907.
42 Letter to Congressman Maurice H. Thatcher, January 7th, 1931. Archives of the Mammoth Cave National Park Association, Western Kentucky University, Bowling Green, Kentucky.
43 Sulzer, Elmer, G., 1958, "The Mammoth Cave Railroad," *The Railroad and Locomotive Historical Society, Bulletin No. 99*. Boston: Baker Library, Harvard Business School, p 37.
44 Personal communication with James H. Richey, great grandson of Aaron Tibbs, January, 2010.
45 Tarbell, David, 1900. *A Trip Through Mammoth Cave*.
46 Slater, John H., about 1917. "Trip to Mammoth Cave." A letter.
47 Schauffler, Robert Haven, 1913, *Romantic America*. New York: Century Company, p 100.
48 Hubbard, Elbert, 1907, *The Philistine*, Vol 25, June, 1907.
49 "Trails End! The Mammoth Cave Railroad, 1886–1931," *The L&N Employees Magazine*, May, 1932, pp 6–7.
50 Smedley, Alfred, 1888, "The Great Mammoth Cave of Kentucky." From his great grandson Patrick Smedley.
51 Sulzer, Elmer G., 1958, "The Mammoth Cave Railroad," *The Railroad and Locomotive Historical Society, Bulletin No. 99*. Boston: Baker library, Harvard Business School, p 36.
52 Sides, Stan. *Diamond Caverns Story*, An unpublished employee training manual.
53 Anonymous, 1870, *Guide Book For The Diamond Cave*, Louisville: *Courier-Journal* Steam Job Print, pp 15, 19.
54 Sides, Stan. *Diamond Caverns Story*, An unpublished employee training manual.
55 Schauffler, Robert Haven, 1913, *Romantic America*. New York: Century Co., p 100.
56 Sides, Stanley D., and Norman Warnell, "Long Cave." An unpublished paper, Cave Research Foundation.
57 *Ibid*.
58 Bird, Robert Montgomery, 1838. *Peter Pilgrim: or a Rambler's Recollections*. Philadelphia: Lea & Blanchard, p 96.
59 Chisholm, T.O., 1892. *Grand Avenue Cave*. Nashville: Brandon

Printing Company, pp 31-32.
60 Sides, Stanley D., and Norman Warnell, "Long Cave." An unpublished paper, Cave Research Foundation.
61 Advertisement for Grand Avenue Cave and Proctors Cave, May 1st, 1889.
62 Chisholm, T.O., 1892, *Grand Avenue Cave*. Nashville: Brandon Printing Company, p 3.
63 Sulzer, Elmer, 1958, "The Mammoth Cave Railroad," *The Railway and Locomotive Historical Society, Bulletin No. 99*. Boston: Harvard Business School, p 38.
64 Randolph, Helen F. *Mammoth Cave and the Cave Region of Kentucky*. Louisville: The Standard Printing Company, pp 113–117,
65 Department of the Interior Bureau of Pensions, Record and Pension Division, War Department document. January 13, 1891.
66 United States Pension Agency document stating Jonathon Doyel's pension was dropped due to death. March 9, 1910.
67 "Proctors Cave," 1891, Mammoth Cave National Park manuscript collection.
68 "Proctors Cave," 1891, Mammoth Cave National Park manuscript collection.
69 Sides, Stanley D., and Norman Warnell, "Long Cave." An un published paper, Cave Research Foundation.
70 Schauffler, Robert Haven, 1913, *Romantic America*. New York: Century Co. pp 100-101.
71 "Knights of Pythias Biennial Conclave," Brochure printed by Passenger Department, L&N Railroad, Louisville, 1904. Edmonson County Court House, Brownsville, Kentucky.
72 "Louisville Public School Children's Day at Mammoth Cave," *The Mammoth Cave Magazine,* Vol 1, No. 2, November, 1912, pp 10–11, 20.
73 "Skidoo Day! October 23!" 1908, *The Green and Gold*, Vol VII, No. 1, pp 20-21.
74 Edmonson County Equity Case #1638, bundle # 125. L.J. Proctor vs. Mammoth Cave Railroad, February 13, 1894.
75 Edmonson County Court document, 1885, pp 140–141.
76 Edmonson County Equity Case # 1638, bundle # 125. L.J. Proctor *vs*. Mammoth Cave Railroad, February 13, 1894.
77 Legal agreement between the Mammoth Cave Railroad Company and L.J. Proctor, Edmonson County Courthouse,

Notes

Brownsville, Kentucky.
78 Sulzer, Elmer, 1958, "The Mammoth Cave Railroad," *The Railway and Locomotive Historical Society, Bulletin No. 99*. Boston: Harvard Business School, pp 32–33.
79 Hubbard, Elbert, 1907, *The Philistine*, Vol 25, June, 1907.
80 *Ibid*, p 38.
81 "Automobile Run to Mammoth Cave," New York Times, June 26, 1903, p 10.
82 Gaines, Ray, 1957, "Paper Records Hercules' Passing," *Dailey News*, October 2, 1957.
83 Sulzer, Elmer, 1958, "The Mammoth Cave Railroad," *The Railway and Locomotive Historical Society Bulletin No. 99*. Boston: Harvard Business School, pp 38–39.
84 "'Gay Nineties Rendezvous' Glasgown Junction to Mammoth Cave (Mammoth Cave Railroad)," p 198.
85 Letter from Mammoth Cave National Park Association member Max B. Nahm to Colonel A.B. Cammerer, Associate Director of the National Park Service, April 22, 1931.
86 Sulzer, Elmer, 1958, "The Mammoth Cave Railroad," *The Railway and Locomotive Historical Society, Bulletin No. 99*. Boston: Harvard Business School, pp 38–39.
87 Goode, Cecil E., 1986, *World Wonder Saved, How Mammoth Cave became a National Park*. Mammoth Cave, Kentucky: The Mammoth Cave National Park Association, p 20.
88 Zubrod, George E. "The L&N's Donation to the Mammoth Cave National Park." *Courier-Journal*, June 13, 1933.
89 United States Circuit Court of Appeals, Sixth Circuit. Transcript of Record, Wyatt and Janin *vs*. Mammoth Cave Development Company, 1927, p 44.
90 "History of Mammoth Cave National Park Project," General Manager Mammoth Cave Properties, September 10, 1940.
91 Letters to Congressman John W. Moore, July 7, 1931 and to W.A. Russell, L&N Railroad Company, November 16, 1931, MCNPA Archives, The Kentucky Library, Kentucky Building, WKU, Bowling Green, Kentucky.
92 Letter from M.L. Charlet, Mammoth Cave Superintendent, March 26, 1931. MCNPA Archives, The Kentucky Library, Kentucky Building, WKU, Bowling Green, Kentucky.
93 Personal communication with Drewing's daughter, Sally Beals.
94 Sulzer, Elmer, 1958, "The Mammoth Cave Railroad," *The*

Railway and Locomotive Historical Society, Bulletin No. 99. Boston: Harvard Business School, p 40.
95 Letters between M.L. Charlet, George E. Zubrod, and others, May 29, 1931; June 2, 1931; June 8, 1931; November 13, 1931. MCNPA Archives, The Kentucky Library, Kentucky Building, WKU, Bowling Green, Kentucky.
96 *Ibid*.
97 Personal communication with Nancy Richie, The Kentucky Library, Kentucky Building, WKU, Bowling Green, Kentucky, February, 2010.
98 Introductory Notes, 18 November 2001. Kentucky Railway Museum, New Haven, Kentucky.
99 Cooperative Agreement Between United States department of the Interior National Park Service and Kentucky Railway Museum, Incorporated, 2002.

Index

A

Age, B.H. 27
American Indians 4, 37
An Excursion Through The United States and Canada During the Years 1822–23 5
Asher, Nick 65
automobile 53

B

Baldwin Locomotive Works 13
Baxter, Jere 9
Beals, Sally 65
bear 5
Bell's Tavern 20
Big South Fork Scenic Railway 63
Bird, Robert Mongomery 36
black people 30
Blane, William 5
Bluegrass Scenic Railroad Museum 63
Blutcher 23
B&O Railroad 24
Bowling Green *Daily News* 53
Bowling Green Normal School 57
Bradbury, Jennifer 65
breast-pins 26
Burke, Kate 65

C

Cadiz Railroad 30
Caldwell County Railroad Museum 63

cane reed torches 4
carbide 15
carbide light 15
Cash, Johnny 7
Cave City 19
Cave, Wrights 36
Chapman, Henry 9
Charlet, Landis 27
Charlet, M.L. 56
Charlet, Pete 27, 56
charter 47
Chaumont Post Office 33, 34
Cincinnati 12
Civilian Conservation Corps 55
Coal and Coke Heritage Center 65
coal car 13
Coats, Jessie 33
Coats, Scott 9
coke 11
Cole, Edmund W. 9
Colossal Cavern 10
combination coach 15, 59
Company, Mammoth Cave Construction 9
conductor, railroad 25
Coolidge, Calvin 55
Cooper, Peter 24
couplers 15
cow catchers 14
Croghan, Dr. John 19
Cugnot, Nicolas 22
Cutliff, W.D. 37
Cuyahoga Valley National Park 55

D

Dewly Colliery 23
Diamond Cave 47
Diamond Caverns 33
Diolkos 21

Index

Doyle, Jonathan 40
Doyle, Oliver 17
Drewing, Herman E. 56, 65
dummy engine 11, 27, 56, 59
DuPont Company 5

E

Eakin, J. Hill 9
East End Railway 13
electric street car 12
Emerson, Ralph Waldo 4
engineer, railroad 25
England 23
Ernst, Richard P. 55
Ethiopia 56

F

Federation of Old Cornwall Societies 65
fireman, railroad 27
Ford Model T 53
Fort Worden State Park 12
France, John Newton "Newt" 39
Furlong, Jewell 14, 26

G

Gallup, F.L. 53
Ganter, Henry C. 42
Ganter's Hotel 33, 42
Glasgow Junction 7, 16, 19, 20, 33, 47, 49, 54
Glasgow *Weekly Times* 9
Gloucester & Cheltenham Railway 11
Grand Avenue Cave 33, 36
Grand Avenue Cave, A Description in Detail of One of America's Greatest Natural Wonders 39
Grand Canyon National Park 55
Graves, D.L. 19
Green River 19

gunpowder 5
gypsum 4, 6

H

hand car 15
Hanson, Coy 15, 65
Harlow, J.H. 19
Hart County News 17
Hatcher, Robert 26
headlight 15
Hercules 3, 14, 26, 53, 57
The Historic Rail Park and Train Museum 63
Homfray, Samuel 22
horses 19, 21
Hoskins, R. Taylor 59
hotel 5
Houchin, John 5
Hovey, Horace 11
Hubbard, Elbert 26, 30, 50
Hudson River Railroad 11

I

Isthmus of Corinth 21

J

Jackson, Nicole 65
James, George 26
Jim Crow law 30
Johnson bar 25
Johnson, Mark 60, 65
Junction, Glasgow 9

K

Kelly, Dan 20
Kentucky Cave Railroad Company 47
Kentucky Railway Museum 59, 63, 65

Index

Killingworth Colliery 23
Kistler, Steve 65
Knights of Pythias 43
Knott, James Proctor 17

L

Lacey, E.H. 53
Lacey, L.P. 53
Lacey, R.H. 9, 37, 49
ladders, bonzai 37
Langford, Terry 65
lantern 15
Lea, Overton 9
Lee, J.L. 37
Leek, Candice 65
Lee, Thomas E. 37
Little Alice 37
Lloyd, B.F. 26
L&N Doesn't Stop Here Any More 7
L&N Railroad 7, 10, 41, 47, 54, 55
Long Cave 39
Louisville *Courier-Journal* 9, 25, 37
Louisville Public School Children's Day 44

M

mail delivery 56
Mammoth Cave 33, 43, 50
Mammoth Cave and the Cave Region of Kentucky 40
Mammoth Cave Estate 44, 47, 50, 57
Mammoth Cave Hotel 30, 42, 47
Mammoth Cave National Park 3, 51, 55, 61
Mammoth Cave National Park Association 54, 55
Mammoth Cave Railroad 53, 61
Mammoth Cave Railroad Company 47
Mammoth Cave Transportation Company 56
McCoy, Andy 19
McDaniel, Jim 9
Melville, Herman 4

77

Midler, Bette 36
Moran, Pat 25
mummy 37
Mussolini 56
My Old Kentucky Dinner Train 63

N

Nashville & West Nashville Railroad 13
national park 51, 55
National Railway Historical Society 64
National Register of Historic Places 59
Newcastle 23
New River Gorge National River 55
New York City 11

O

Olson Colleen 3
Olson, Rick 65
Overton, A.M. 9
Owens, Darlene 65

P

Paducah Railroad Museum 64
Park City 7, 33
passenger coach 15
Pease, Edward 23
Penetanguishene Centennial Museum 12, 65
Penydarren Ironworks 22
Peter Pilgrim: or A Rambler's Recollections 36
Philadelphia 12
The Philistine 50
Pike, Carol 65
Pit Cave 36
Potter College 45
Pritchard, George 65
Proctor Cave 36, 40, 47
Proctor, George 36

Proctor, James 41
Proctor, Larkin J. 9, 36
Proctor, Mary 36
Proctor's Hotel 33, 36, 40
Puffing Devil 22
Pulliam, Annie 17

R

railbus 54
Railroad, Mammoth Cave 9
Randolph, Helen F. 40
R.H. Lacy 39
Richardson, W.F. 17
Richey, James 65
Richey, Nancy 65
riverboats 19
Robert Stephenson & Company 24
Rolling Ford River Valley 63
Romantic America 30

S

saltpeter 5
Salts Cave 37
sand 26
Schauffler, Robert Haven 30
Scientific American 11
Seighman, Pamela 65
Seymour, Tres 65
Sharlot Hall Museum 12, 65
Slater, John H. 29
Sloans Crossing 33, 42
Smedley, Alfred 3Smith, Milton 55
Spence, David 65
stagecoach 7, 19
stalactites 29
stalagmites 29
steam locomotives 61
Steamtown National Historic Site 55

Stephenson, George 23
Stephenson, Robert 24
Stockton & Darlington Railway Company 23
Stockton & Stokes Stagecoach Company 24
Stone, Debbie 65

T

tank engine 12
Tarbell, David 29
tender 13
The Women's Club 51
Thomas's Massachusetts Spy 5
Thomas the Tank Engine 12
Thompson, Lee 53
Tibbs, Aaron 27, 65
Tissandier, Albert 19
Tomlin, Lily 36
Tom Thumb 24
trains 61
Trevithick, Richard 22
A Trip Through Mammoth Cave 29
turnout 49

U

Union City 15, 33, 39

V

Verne, Jules 4

W

Warnell, Normal 65
War of 1812 5
Washington Post 17
Waterman, Henry 11
Western Kentucky University 45, 57
Whitney, J.B. 26

Index

Woodcock, Mick 65
Woods, Wondering 36
Wood, Virgil 27
world's longest cave 4
World War I 29
Wright, W.W. 36
wye 16

Y

Yakel, John 65

Z

Zubrod, George E. 57